Contents

About this book

Writing stories

This book is designed to help young children develop their skills as story-tellers and story-writers. Before children can successfully write stories of their own, they need to absorb the language, rhythm, pattern and shape of existing stories by listening to them. Those with a simple, predictable story line, told in direct language and with repeating sequences, such as those in this book, are particularly helpful.

The book is organised as six pairs of linked double pages. On the first double page is an illustrated story to read aloud: a re-telling of a well-known traditional tale or rhyme, or a new story that has been written with a simple structure for children to follow. In several cases, the narrative structure is supported by repetitive phrases and sequences. Children can draw upon the examples featured throughout the book to create their own stories.

The great big ENORMOUS turnip
by Alexei Tolstoy

Once upon a time,
an old man planted a little turnip.
He said, 'Grow, little turnip, grow sweet and strong.'
The turnip grew sweet and strong and big. It grew ENORMOUS
One day, the old man went to pull it up.
He pulled and he tugged, but he couldn't pull it up.

He called
the old woman.

The old woman pulled the old man.
The old man pulled the turnip.
They pulled and they tugged,
but they couldn't pull it up.

The old woman
called her granddaughter.

The granddaughter pulled the old woman.
The old woman pulled the old man.
The old man pulled the turnip.
They pulled and they tugged,
but they couldn't pull it up.

The granddaughter
called the dog.

The dog pulled the granddaughter.
The granddaughter pulled the old woman.
The old woman pulled the old man.
The old man pulled the turnip.
They pulled and they tugged,
but they couldn't pull it up.

The dog called the cat.

The cat pulled the dog.
The dog pulled the granddaughter.
The granddaughter pulled the old woman.
The old woman pulled the old man.
The old man pulled the turnip.
They pulled and they tugged,
but they still couldn't pull it up.

The cat called the mouse.

The mouse pulled the cat.
The cat pulled the dog.
The dog pulled the granddaughter.
The granddaughter pulled the old woman.
The old woman pulled the old man.
The old man pulled the turnip.
They pulled and pulled again,
and guess what?

The turnip popped

out of the ground.

The old woman cut up the turnip and made it into soup.
Then everyone came to eat it.

6

7

Alternative main characters

Other alternative characters

IT'S ENORMOUS
Write your own story about an enormous vegetable.
★ What is it?   ★ Who planted it?

a potato   a carrot
a radish   a parsnip   a farmer   a gardener   a giant

A story opening phrase

★ Begin your story like this:
  Once upon a time . . .

A repetitive pattern

★ What happened when he tried to pull the vegetable up?
  He pulled and he tugged, but . . .
★ Who came to help?

a rhinoceros   an elephant   a bear

★ Who came to help as well?

a lion   a tiger   a donkey

8

★ Who came to help next?

a boy   a girl   a monkey
★ Who came to help after that?

a frog   a duck   a tortoise
★ Who came to help, last of all?

a rat   a hamster   a mole
★ What happened to the enormous vegetable?

They cut it up and gave everyone a bit.   They made a big stew.

9

A choice of endings

The second double page provides young writers either with guidance on writing their own version of a story, or gives suggestions and choices for them to create their own piece of writing, based on the existing story or rhyme. The instructions give children a clear, step-by-step framework for a story or rhyme, identifying and illustrating the main incidents from start to finish.

Of course, once children are confident with these tales, they may prefer to use them just as springboards to invent their own stories, choosing their own characters and events.

Useful words
The pull-out flap provides an alphabetical list of common words, which children may find helpful to use while writing their stories.

Encouraging story writing
There are suggestions about how best to help and inspire children to write stories on pages 30 and 31. These, in turn, may prompt you to devise other ideas of your own. Encourage children to use the language of story writing throughout their stories, eg One day … There was once … At that moment … The next morning … When evening came … In the end … At last ….

Reminders for writing
There are some hints about the use of story-writing language and reminders about using punctuation, capital letters and connecting words on page 32.

The great big ENORMOUS turnip
by Alexei Tolstoy

Once upon a time,
an old man planted a little turnip.
He said, 'Grow, little turnip, grow sweet and strong.'
The turnip grew sweet and strong and big. It grew ENORMOUS.
One day, the old man went to pull it up.
He pulled and he tugged, but he couldn't pull it up.

He called
the old woman.

The old woman pulled the old man.
The old man pulled the turnip.
They pulled and they tugged,
but they couldn't pull it up.

The old woman
called her granddaughter.

The granddaughter pulled the old woman.
The old woman pulled the old man.
The old man pulled the turnip.
They pulled and they tugged,
but they couldn't pull it up.

The granddaughter
called the dog.

The dog pulled the granddaughter.
The granddaughter pulled the old woman.
The old woman pulled the old man.
The old man pulled the turnip.
They pulled and they tugged,
but they couldn't pull it up.

The dog called the cat.

The cat pulled the dog.
The dog pulled the granddaughter.
The granddaughter pulled the old woman.
The old woman pulled the old man.
The old man pulled the turnip.
They pulled and they tugged,
but they still couldn't pull it up.

The cat called the mouse.

The mouse pulled the cat.
The cat pulled the dog.
The dog pulled the granddaughter.
The granddaughter pulled the old woman.
The old woman pulled the old man.
The old man pulled the turnip.
They pulled and pulled again,
and guess what?
The turnip p^{o}pped

out of the ground.

The old woman cut up the turnip and made it into soup.
Then everyone came to eat it.

It's Enormous

Write your own story about an enormous vegetable.

★ **What is it?**

a potato

a carrot

a radish

a parsnip

★ **Who planted it?**

a farmer

a gardener

a giant

★ **Begin your story like this:**

Once upon a time . . .

★ **What happened when he tried to pull the vegetable up?**

He pulled and he tugged, but . . .

★ **Who came to help?**

a rhinoceros

an elephant

a bear

★ **Who came to help as well?**

a lion

a tiger

a donkey

★ Who came to help next?

a boy

a girl

a monkey

★ Who came to help after that?

a frog

a duck

a tortoise

★ Who came to help, last of all?

a rat

a hamster

a mole

★ What happened to the enormous vegetable?

They cut it up and gave everyone a bit.

They made a big stew.

Our new puppy

On Monday,
Mum gave us a new puppy.
We named him Zipper.

On Tuesday,
we played with Zipper in the garden
and he dug up Dad's roses.

On Wednesday,
we took Zipper for a walk
and he left muddy footprints all over the kitchen.

On Thursday,
we played with Zipper upstairs
and he chewed my sister's new shoes.

On Friday,
Mum said, 'That dog is too much trouble.'
She swapped him for a goldfish.

On Saturday,
we sat and watched the goldfish.
It was boring. Goldfish are no fun at all.

On Sunday,
Mum brought Zipper back.
Next week, we're going to start training him.

MY NEW PET

Imagine you have a new kitten. Write about a week with your new pet.

On Monday...

miaowed

curled

ate

On Tuesday...

stretched

sat

played

On Wednesday...

jumped

sniffed

climbed

On Thursday…

hid

caught

licked

On Friday…

stalked

patted

rolled

On Saturday…

pounced

spilt

scratched

★ **What happened on Sunday?**

On Sunday…

The princess and the pea

Based on the story by Hans Christian Anderson

There was once a prince who wanted to marry a princess – a real princess. He travelled far and wide looking for one. On his way, he met plenty of princesses, but there was something wrong with them all. Some were too young and some were too old. Some talked too much and some didn't talk at all. Some ate too much and others laughed too much. In the end, he went home again feeling very sad.

One evening, soon after his return, there was a terrible storm. Lightning cracked, thunder crashed and rain poured down in buckets. Suddenly, there was a loud knock at the palace door. The king went to open it. A shivering girl huddled on the doorstep. What a mess she looked! Water streamed down her face and hair, and her clothes were muddy and soaking.

'I'm a princess, looking for shelter,' she said softly. 'The wheel of my coach is broken and it can't be mended until tomorrow.'

'A princess?' murmured the queen to herself, 'We'll soon find out about that.'

While the girl warmed herself by the fire, the queen went to prepare a bedroom for her. She sent her maids all over the palace to fetch mattresses and quilts. First, she placed a hard, dried pea on the base of the bed and then piled twenty mattresses on top of it. After that, she piled twenty feather quilts on top of the mattresses.

Then the princess went to bed.

In the morning, the king and queen asked the princess how she had slept.

'I hardly slept a wink all night,' she replied. 'I was lying on something so hard that I'm bruised black and blue all over.'

The king and queen were delighted to hear this, for only a real princess could have felt a tiny pea through twenty mattresses and twenty feather quilts. The prince was overjoyed too, for he knew that at last he had found a *real* princess to marry. As for the pea, it was put on show in the royal museum where it can still be seen today, unless someone has taken it.

TELL THE STORY

Re-tell the story of the princess and the pea.
Use the pictures to help you.

★ Begin the story.

★ What happened?

★ What happened next?

★ What happened in the end?

★ What happened to the pea?

There was an old lady

There was an old lady who swallowed a fly.
I don't know why she swallowed a fly –
        Perhaps she'll die.

There was an old lady who swallowed a spider
That wriggled and wiggled and jiggled inside her.

She swallowed the spider to catch the fly.
I don't know why she swallowed a fly –
        Perhaps she'll die.

There was an old lady who swallowed a bird.
How absurd to swallow a bird!

She swallowed the bird to catch the spider.
She swallowed the spider to catch the fly.
I don't know why she swallowed a fly –
        Perhaps she'll die.

There was an old lady who swallowed a cat.
Now fancy that! She swallowed a cat.

She swallowed the cat to catch the bird.
She swallowed the bird to catch the spider.
She swallowed the spider to catch the fly.
I don't know why she swallowed a fly –
        Perhaps she'll die.

There was an old lady who swallowed a dog.
Oh, what a hog to swallow a dog!

She swallowed the dog to catch the cat.
She swallowed the cat to catch the bird.
She swallowed the bird to catch the spider.
She swallowed the spider to catch the fly.
I don't know why she swallowed a fly –
        Perhaps she'll die.

There was an old lady who swallowed a goat.
She just opened her mouth and it went down her throat.

She swallowed the goat to catch the dog.
She swallowed the dog to catch the cat.
She swallowed the cat to catch the bird.
She swallowed the bird to catch the spider.
She swallowed the spider to catch the fly.
I don't know why she swallowed a fly –
              Perhaps she'll die.

There was an old lady who swallowed a cow.
I don't know how she swallowed a cow.

She swallowed the cow to catch the goat.
She swallowed the goat to catch the dog.
She swallowed the dog to catch the cat.
She swallowed the cat to catch the bird.
She swallowed the bird to catch the spider.
She swallowed the spider to catch the fly.
I don't know why she swallowed a fly –
              Perhaps she'll die.

There was an old lady
who swallowed a horse.
            She died, of course!

A STORY RHYME

Make up your own rhyme about the old lady.
Choose one thing for each new verse.

★ There was an old lady who swallowed a...

 flea   pea    bee

I really can't see why she swallowed a...
   Perhaps it's her tea.

★ There was an old lady who swallowed a...

 bug    slug    mug

With a gluggity-glug, she swallowed a...

★ There was an old lady who swallowed a...

 hat    bat    rat

Just like that, she swallowed a...

★ There was an old lady who swallowed a...

 brick    stick   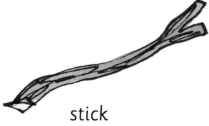 chick

For her next trick, she swallowed a...

★ There was an old lady who swallowed a...

clock

cock

sock

She stood on a rock and just swallowed a...

★ There was an old lady who swallowed a...

snake

cake

rake

She sat by a lake and swallowed a...

★ There was an old lady who swallowed a yak.
Now she needs a thwack on the...

21

The man, the boy and the donkey

One day, a man and his son decided to take their donkey to market. They set off, leading the donkey on a rope. They hadn't gone far when they passed a field and a farmer said to them, 'You're silly. Why are you both walking when one of you could ride?'

'He's right,' thought the man.

He got on to the donkey and rode along with his son beside him. As they passed a cottage in the woods, an old woman exclaimed to the man, 'You're horrid. Why are you riding that donkey while your little son has to run to keep up with you? Let him ride instead.'

'She's right,' thought the man.

He got off the donkey and his son got on instead. When they came to a crossroads, a man complained to the boy, 'You're lazy. Why are you riding that donkey when your father has to walk? You should both ride.'

'He's right,' thought the man and got on to the donkey behind his son.

They rode on until they reached the edge of town. As they passed a shop, a shopkeeper shouted to them, 'You're cruel. Why are you both riding that donkey? Can't you see that it's exhausted?'

'He's right,' thought the man.

He and the boy got off the donkey and thought about what to do next. Then the man had an idea. He cut a long pole and tied the donkey's feet to it with rope. He and the boy slung the pole over their shoulders and carried the donkey through the streets.

How people laughed at them!

'You're fools!' they cried, 'Why are you carrying that donkey when it could perfectly well walk?'

By this time, the man and the boy had almost reached market. They were just crossing the bridge over a river when, all of a sudden, the donkey started twitching and thrashing to get free. It fell into the river with a splish and a splash and was never seen again.

'Oh dear,' sighed the man. 'I tried to listen to everybody, but I shouldn't have listened to anybody.'

A STORY MAP

Follow the journey that the man, the boy and their donkey took to market on this story map.

Start

house

field

wood

cottage

crossroads

shops

town

bridge

The end

The end

market

Draw your own story map to help plan
a story about the man, the boy and their donkey.

★ Where do they start?

a house

a castle

a farm

a cave

★ Where do they go – first, next and last?

a forest

a city

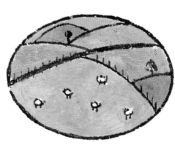
fields

a shopping mall

★ Whom do they meet?

a woodcutter

a shopkeeper

a gardener

a fisherman

a road sweeper

a flower seller

★ Use your story map to tell the story.

Midas and his golden touch

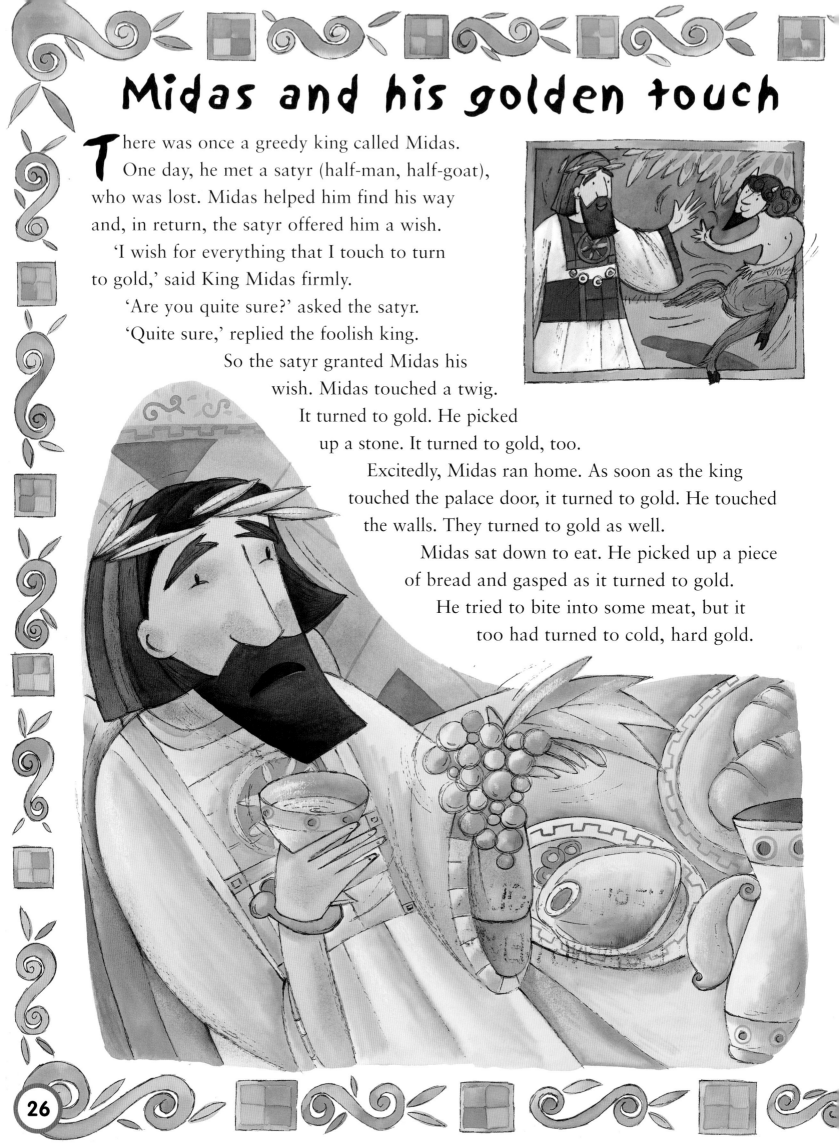

There was once a greedy king called Midas. One day, he met a satyr (half-man, half-goat), who was lost. Midas helped him find his way and, in return, the satyr offered him a wish.

'I wish for everything that I touch to turn to gold,' said King Midas firmly.

'Are you quite sure?' asked the satyr.

'Quite sure,' replied the foolish king.

So the satyr granted Midas his wish. Midas touched a twig. It turned to gold. He picked up a stone. It turned to gold, too.

Excitedly, Midas ran home. As soon as the king touched the palace door, it turned to gold. He touched the walls. They turned to gold as well.

Midas sat down to eat. He picked up a piece of bread and gasped as it turned to gold. He tried to bite into some meat, but it too had turned to cold, hard gold.

He reached for some wine, but that turned into liquid gold before he could take a sip.

Just then his young daughter came running in and gave him a big hug.

'No!' cried King Midas, but it was too late. His daughter had turned into a silent, still, gold statue.

By this time, Midas felt very hungry, very thirsty and very sad. He hurried into the woods to find the satyr.

'Please take back my wish,' he begged.

'Very well,' said the satyr. 'Go and wash yourself all over in the river. Maybe you won't make such a foolish wish another time.'

Midas dived into the river and washed himself all over. The river began to sparkle with gold dust. Midas was soon cured.

He rushed home and poured river water over his daughter.

When she came back to life again, Midas hugged and kissed her. He never made a foolish wish again.

A MAGIC WISH

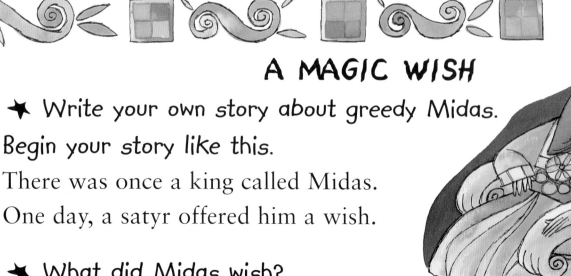

★ Write your own story about greedy Midas.
Begin your story like this.

There was once a king called Midas.
One day, a satyr offered him a wish.

★ What did Midas wish?

Midas said, 'I want everything that I touch to turn to …

silver

diamonds

chocolate

chips

★ What did Midas touch? What happened to it?

leaf

berries

flower

bush

★ What did Midas touch next? What happened to it?

chair

table

picture

window

carpet

bed

curtains

fireplace

★ What happened when Midas sat down to eat?

grapes   cake   chicken   melon   apple   fish   pear

★ Who came to see Midas? What happened?

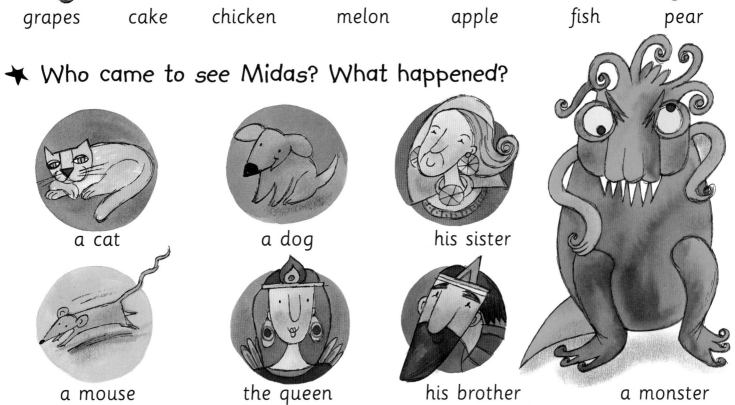

a cat   a dog   his sister

a mouse   the queen   his brother   a monster

★ How did Midas feel? What did he do?

★ What did the satyr tell him to do?

stand under a waterfall

dive to the seabed

have a bubble bath

drink a magic potion

★ What did Midas say and do? What happened in the end?

More writing ideas

Telling and re-telling well-known tales

You will need to re-tell stories over and over again before children know them well enough to internalise the language patterns and structures.

✦ Emphasise particular words, use gestures and mime actions (eg pulling up the turnip) in your storytelling to help signal key events.

✦ Encourage children to join in with the repetitive parts.

✦ Pause at dramatic moments to give children opportunities to tell some of the tale for themselves.

✦ You may find it useful to tell the stories on to tape, so that children can listen to them at their own pace.

In their own words

All the stories in this book are highly illustrated. Children can use the illustrations as useful prompts to re-tell the stories themselves, either orally or by writing them down.

Children can create their own storyboard of a tale, picking out key events to illustrate and caption.

Pages 16–17, which re-tell the story of *The princess and the pea* in a storyboard format, provide an example which the children can follow.

Story maps

Drawing a story map of a well-known tale, especially one which involves a journey, such as *Chicken Licken, Little Red Riding Hood, The Three Little Pigs* or *The Gingerbread Man*, is a useful way visually to show the framework of the entire story. Page 24 shows an example. Children can make a story map as a planner for their own journey story. Before they start, talk about:

* who is going on the journey
* why they are going
* where their characters will start from and where they are going to
* whom they meet on the way
* what happens
* where they end up

Children can then plot the route their characters follow, draw the places they go to along the way and other characters that they meet, and add labels and captions.

Acting out a story

By presenting a story as a play, either dressing-up, making paper-bag or stick puppets, or using dolls or toy animals, children have a chance to discuss the story together and become familiar with its structure by acting out its events.

Changing a story

When children know a story really well, perhaps even by heart, then you can introduce the idea of changing it – using its underlying framework for a new story, adding or dropping characters, changing the settings, including new incidents and altering the ending. *There was an old lady* on pages 18–21, *The great, big, enormous turnip* on pages 6–9, *Our new puppy* on pages 10–13 and *Midas and his golden touch* on pages 26–29 offer some suggestions for doing this. Use these ideas to adapt other stories in a similar way.

Story-writing hints

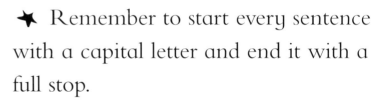

★ Think about the words you will use to begin your story, eg

> There was once …
> One day …
> Long, long ago …

★ Remember to start every sentence with a capital letter and end it with a full stop.

> A shivering girl stood on the doorstep.

★ Say what happened in order. Use words such as first, then, after that.

> First, she placed a hard, dried pea on the base of the bed and then piled twenty mattresses on top of it. After that, she piled twenty feather quilts on top of the mattresses.

★ Start a question with a capital letter and end it with a question mark.

> Why are you both riding that donkey?

★ Think about the words you could use to end your story, eg

> Finally …
> In the end …
> At last …

★ Read through what you have written. Make any changes you think would improve your story. Check for capital letters, full stops and question marks.